GW01375203

Kingfisher Books, Grisewood & Dempsey Ltd,
Elsley House, 24-30 Great Titchfield Street,
London W1P 7AD

First published in 1993 by Kingfisher Books
2 4 6 8 10 9 7 5 3 1

Material in this edition was previously published by
Kingfisher Books in *Animal Life Stories: The Penguin*
in 1988 and in *Wildlife Library: The Penguin* in 1978.

© Grisewood & Dempsey Ltd 1978, 1988, 1993

All rights reserved
British Library Cataloguing in Publication Data
A catalogue record for this book is available from
the British Library
ISBN 1 85697 084 1

Series editor: Veronica Pennycook
Series designer: Terry Woodley
Cover illustration by Steve Holden/John Martin & Artists
Illustrations on pp 6-7 & 12-13 by Steve Lings/Linden Artists
Typeset in 3B2
Phototypeset by SPAN
Printed in Great Britain by
BPCC Paulton Books Limited

LITTLE LIBRARY

The Emperor Penguin

Angela Royston
Illustrated by Trevor Boyer

Kingfisher Books

In this book

The penguins in this story are emperor penguins. They live in the cold Antarctic, near the South Pole.

- Sharp bill
- The crop is a pocket inside the throat where the penguin stores food
- Flippers for swimming
- Strong claws to grip the icy ground

Emperor

King

There are 18 kinds of penguin and they all live in the southern half of the world. Five of the different kinds, from the largest to the smallest, are shown here.

Penguins cannot fly and do not move very well on land, but they are excellent swimmers.

Adelie   Rockhopper   Little blue

A narrow escape

The penguin swims through the clear, icy water. Every now and again he dives down to catch a fish or a squid. Then suddenly he sees a huge dark shape gliding swiftly towards him through the water. It's a hungry killer whale.

The penguin swims for his life, beating his flippers against the water as fast as he can. He leaps out of the water on to the ice just ahead of the whale's jaws.

Finding a mate

Winter has arrived and the penguin is fat and sleek after a summer of feeding in the sea.

Now he is ready to mate and it's time to set off inland to the penguins' breeding grounds.

There, a chattering crowd of emperor penguins gathers. The male penguin joins them.

He stands turning his head from side to side to show off his bright orange neck. A female waddles over. She will be his mate.

A single egg

Four weeks later the female penguin lays a single egg. She has no nest to keep the egg warm so she carefully passes it to her mate to look after. The male tucks the precious egg under a fold of skin just above his feet.

Now that the female knows her mate will keep the egg warm and safe, she starts off back to the sea.

Meanwhile, the male carefully carries the egg on his feet as he waddles into a large group with some of the other males.

Winter storms

The male penguin has not eaten since leaving the sea. But he has plenty of fat on his body to keep him going until his mate returns.

Even so, guarding the egg is not easy. Snow swirls around the penguins and strong, icy winds blow day after day. For two months the male penguins huddle together, guarding their eggs and keeping them warm.

The egg hatches

One day the egg cracks and breaks open. A hungry little chick is soon sitting on his father's feet.

The male penguin still has a little food left in his stomach and he feeds this to the chick. But it won't last very long and he looks anxiously for the mother to come back from the sea.

Help arrives

At last a plump
female comes
waddling
towards them
across the
windswept ice.

She greets her mate and the chick moves on to her feet. Then the mother opens her beak and the little chick starts to feed.

Off to the sea

The male penguins are thin and hungry after the long winter. They set off at once for the sea, sometimes walking, sometimes sliding on their bellies.

Luckily the sea is not so far away now. Spring has come and the ice is melting. The tired male penguin slides into the water. But he cannot stay long. As soon as he is fat again he fills his crop with food and trails back over the ice to feed his chick.

Danger!

The chick is soon big enough to leave his parents' feet, but he feels cold and scared on his own. As he shuffles across the ice to join a huddle of other chicks, a huge seabird swoops down towards him.

The tiny, frightened penguin skates on his belly and the group of chicks lets him into the safety of the huddle. The little penguin will only leave this group when one of his parents comes back from the sea with food for him.

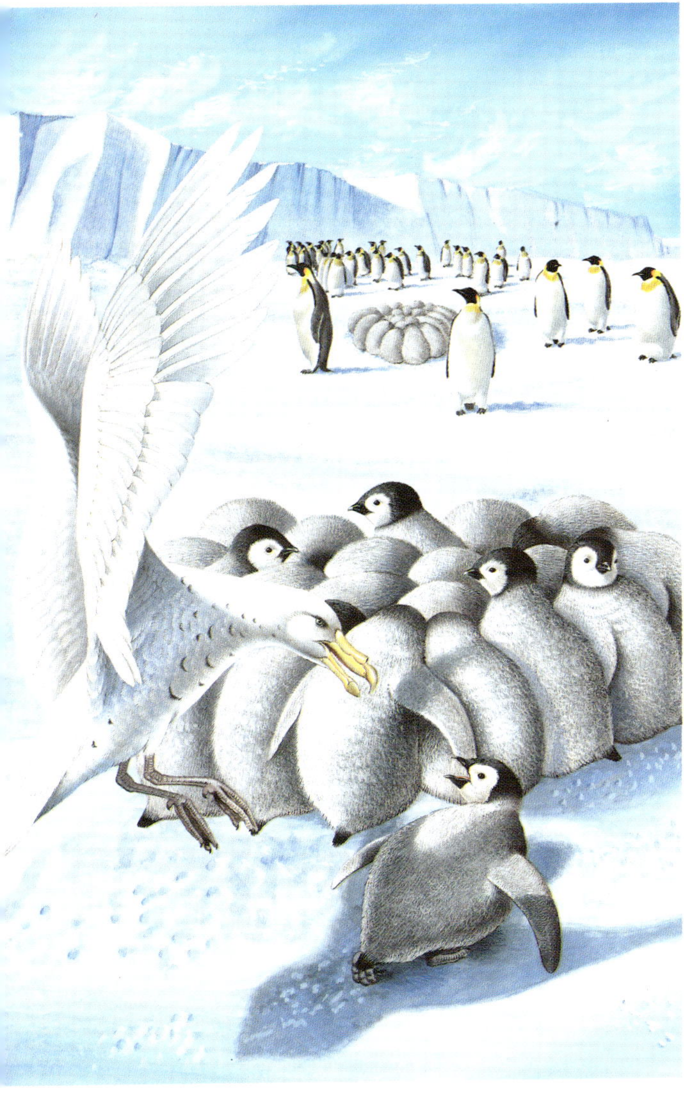

Growing up

As the weather gets warmer and the young penguin grows bigger, he slowly loses his soft, fluffy feathers. With his new sleek waterproof coat he is ready to go to the sea.

When all the chicks in his huddle have their new coats they set off down to the sea together.

Soon they come to the edge of the ice. The sea below looks strange and dangerous.

All the young penguins are very hungry. Finally, one of them dives in to feed on the fish. The others quickly follow.

Watching for danger

A leopard seal has been watching the penguins from the ice. She slips smoothly into the water and catches a young penguin.

From then on all the young penguins watch out for enemies.

As summer passes, the young penguin becomes a good swimmer. He stays in the sea, feeding on fish and squid.

Then winter comes and, like his parents, he makes the long trek inland to find a mate.

Some special words

Antarctic A large area of ice-covered land surrounding the South Pole. It is the coldest place on Earth.

Huddle When chicks first leave their parents' feet they often crowd together in huddles. This helps to keep them warm and safe from attack by birds who might try to snatch a chick if it was on its own.

Leopard seal These seals are the penguins' main enemy. They catch the penguins just as they dive into the water. Once they are swimming, adult penguins can usually escape.

Squid A sea creature with long tentacles.

Index

chick   16, 19, 24, 28
crop   6, 21
egg flap   12
feathers   24
fish   8, 25, 27
flippers   6, 9
huddle   15, 22, 23, 28
leopard seal   26, 28
squid   8, 27, 28